This Book Belongs to:

....

....

JUDO for Kids Coloring Book

Copyright © 2020 by S.S. Publishing
All rights reserved. No part of this book may be reproduced or used in any manner without written permission of the copyright owner except for the use of quotations in a book review.

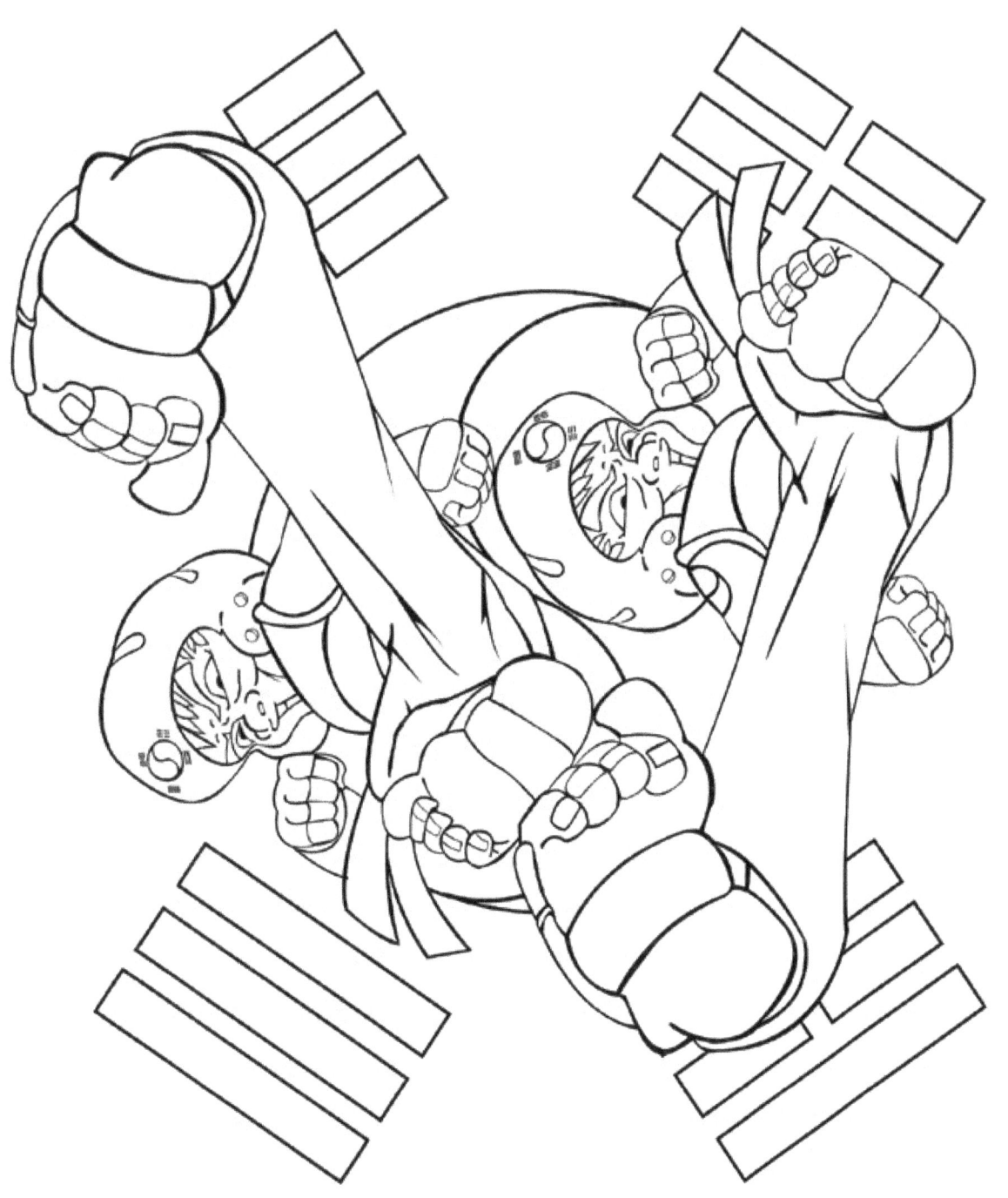

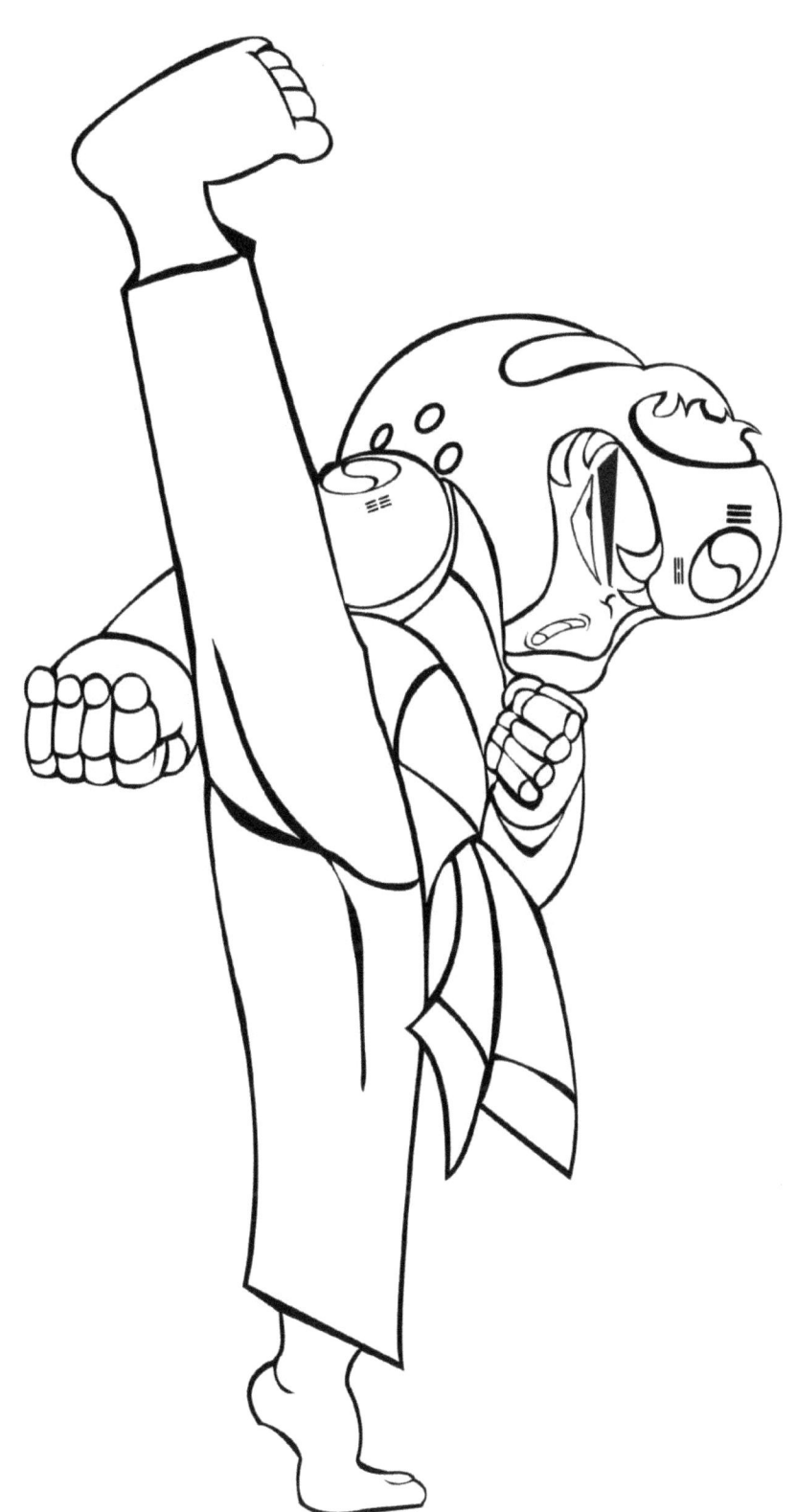

Milton Keynes UK
Ingram Content Group UK Ltd.
UKHW031900041223
433765UK00017B/1314